HEALTHY H

The authors of this book sweep
and set forth a natural plan
hair growth. They deal with both common and not
so common disorders of the hair and scalp, and give
a message of hope to those developing baldness.

HEALTHY HAIR

Care and restoration by natural methods

by
JAMES C. THOMSON
and
C. LESLIE THOMSON, B.Sc.
of the Kingston Clinic, Edinburgh

NATURE'S WAY

THORSONS PUBLISHERS LIMITED
Wellingborough, Northamptonshire

First published as *Hair and Scalp
Disorders including Baldness,* 1932
(Six Impressions)
Rewritten Edition retitled
How to Obtain Healthy Hair, 1939
(Sixteen Impressions)
Revised Edition 1962
New Edition, completely revised and enlarged, 1967
Second Impression 1969
First paperback Edition, 1972
Sixth Impression 1983
First published this Edition 1986

ISBN 0 7225 0377 6

Printed and bound in Great Britain by
Richard Clay (The Chaucer Press) Ltd.,
Bungay, Suffolk

FOREWORD

My father's original book was an immediate success when it first appeared 35 years ago. It continued to give encouragement and effective advice to its readers through 24 reprintings. This edition—the twenty-fifth printing—has been completely rewritten and considerably extended, but it preserves the essential sequence and logic of the original author's message.

Kingston, Edinburgh, 9.   **C.L.T.**

CONTENTS

CHAPTER I

HAIR FUNCTION AND GROWTH

THE Kingston System is founded upon the belief that the correct treatment for any ailment or disorder must depend upon a thorough understanding of the major factors and difficulties involved. It is not enough to diagnose the condition correctly; there must also be an appreciation of the causes which have gone before and of the practical necessities for producing an improvement. Too often it is assumed that, once a condition has been named, the remedial treatment may be automatically prescribed —a misunderstanding which is sustained by much of the advertising for proprietary medicaments. This situation applies just as much to healthy hair growth—or rather to *lack* of healthy hair growth— as to any of the more vitally serious ailments of human kind.

Possibly the most important feature to be noted about hair is that its primary function is protective. It is there to save other, more delicate and more vital, tissues from injury. So it is that when we look closely at the hair roots we find an assembly of structures and mechanisms which assist the hair to protect the scalp and the head as a whole; the main threats to these being thermal shock and mechanical impact. We may observe the protective devices in action very clearly in a dog or cat ready for a fight. The hair stands out in a bristling and resilient layer of armour. Although less visible to the onlooker, the same phenomenon occurs in man when he is frightened. He may feel a prickling of the scalp, and we say that "his hair stands on end". This is quite literally true if his terror is intense. The effect of cold upon the hairs is more noticeable on the limbs and trunk, where the numerous tiny muscular exertions produce "goose-flesh". On the scalp, where the hairs are normally far more closely arranged, the individual responses are concealed.

Not too Careful

Few people are properly informed about how hair grows, and what its normal functions are, so that many fallacious beliefs are prevalent. Of these, one which we commonly encounter is that a thinning hair-growth should be delicately handled. But since we have already accepted that hair is itself a protective structure, it should be logically obvious that there is nothing to fear in handling it fairly vigorously. No matter how the advertisements for hair preparations may suggest that it should be treated like a delicate plant, we cannot accept such implications as being physiologically justified. Indeed, it is our finding that the more the hair is pampered and protected, the more hopeless are the prospects of any improvement in its quality and vigour.

There is a rule which has been observed to apply to all the working parts of the human body. In simple terms, any tissue which is not called upon to perform its proper purpose, regularly and vigorously, loses its capacity for that function. Initially, it weakens a little; gradually it degenerates, and in the end it becomes inert and may be absorbed. If this happens to a vital organ, the individual also dies. If the tissue is not essential to the body's needs, the owner is not usually seriously affected; but if the structures are relatively small, they tend to be obliterated. And this is what may happen if, through having not enough to do, the hair "roots" are allowed to fall into a devitalised state.

The essential function of the hair is protective. Therefore, to produce a stronger and healthier growth of hair, the individual's habits must be altered so as to call for protection more frequently and with greater intensity as time passes. But although that is one essential step, it must also be understood that individual characteristics and needs may call for considerable modification in method of treatment. There may be such complicating factors as hereditary weaknesses, abnormal development of the hair follicles (the tiny pits in which the hair is formed) or a more or less severe degree of degeneration within the scalp. Even so, the principle is unaltered, and with individually-adjusted applications to stimulate sturdier hair growth, a healthier and more natural response may be looked for.

Call to Action

It is never too early to begin cultivation of strong hair growth. The sooner the basic principles are understood and acted upon, the more probable is the maintenance of a healthy head of hair right through life. A growth of hair which is still vigorous and in good condition may be relatively easily maintained. By the time the hair follicles have begun to lose their mature fullness, becoming shrivelled and inactive, it will require many months of patient work to produce even a slight improvement. There is no need for any truly normal and healthy head of hair ever to become sparse. All that is necessary is to insist upon it doing its proper work. The demand should be vigorous, positive and frequent.

To give some idea of what we mean by vigorous, here is a little anecdote with which James C. Thomson used to illustrate the point:

"On one of my visits to the USSR, I witnessed a good-humoured struggle between two Russian deck-hands. One of them was a muscular woman who, with a few quick movements, laid her able-bodied male opponent on his back solely by her grip on his hair. Most men would call that a foul: most women would say that such treatment was good for the man's character. My own response would be different from both; I would say that it was excellent for the man's hair. Indeed, the incident suggests to me a healthful, interesting and spectacular form of exercise. I suggest the

organisation of hair-wrestling as a national—
even international—sport."

(James C. Thomson himself often used to chal-
lenge patients who consulted him about failing hair
to grasp and tug his own hair as vigorously as they
pleased. He also entertained children by having
two of them hang from his hair—one on either side—
then turning about to make a living merry-go-
round.)

The "Hair Food" Fallacy

Hair is produced by cells which are part of the
skin, of the same kind as the living layer of the skin
but modified into special structures known as
follicles. Whereas the general epithelial cells produce
a more or less flat layer of dead, horny, surface skin,
the specialised cells produce the characteristic shafts
or cylinders of solid tissue—the hairs. In the human,
hair is produced—to a greater or lesser extent—
over the whole body with the exception of the palms
of the hands, the soles of the feet and one or two
smaller areas. Over most of the body, the hairs are
tiny; called lanugo, they are short, almost colourless
and downy in character. On the head, eyebrows
and eyelids—as well as in other areas—they attain
a much higher grade of development, becoming
thicker and longer under normal conditions as the
person grows older.

But wherever situated, and however strong the
growth, the hair itself is a dead substance, projected

from the tiny pits of living cells within the skin. Within the follicles, the hair substance dies as it is produced—the process occurring within what is called the "root" of the hair. This is the slightly swollen, rough-surfaced and not-quite-hardened end which is exposed when a healthy hair is tweaked out of its follicle. Once the hair leaves the follicle —in the process of normal growth—it is totally inert, with neither growth nor nourishment taking place. It is extended purely by the continuing formation of new tissue within the follicle.

These points have been deliberately stressed, because they hold the key to proper understanding of what is involved in promoting healthy hair. They should also make it quite clear that nothing rubbed into the exposed hair—or "fed into its stalk"—can increase its health or vitality to the slightest degree. The stalk portion is no longer capable of improvement or of growth, and therefore cannot be nourished.

Formation

Nor can the follicles be "nourished" from substances rubbed on to the skin. The follicles have no mechanism for digesting or absorbing nutrients from without. The only way to nourish the hair is *during its formation* by ensuring proper supplies of nutrients in the blood which feeds the follicles. In the area we are considering, it means that there must be an adequate circulation of good blood to the scalp. The rubbing of foodstuffs into the shaft or around the roots of the hair cannot improve its growth, health or durability. No matter how excellent the applied substance may be as a nutrient when eaten and digested in the normal way, it is utterly useless when put on the scalp. (It may, perhaps, save misunderstanding to point out that some oily and greasy substances can give the hair a glossier appearance which may resemble the natural sheen of healthy hair, but without its accompanying quality.) And there are food substances which, if applied to the scalp, may damage the hair or cause irritation of the skin.

Once the hair shaft—or stalk—has grown out of its follicle, even the blood cannot affect it. The blood nourishes the follicle, which in turn produces the root, but no part of the blood reaches beyond the root up into the shaft. This point, too, is worth emphasis because it is easy to imagine that hair is analogous to grass, with sap rising through the stem from the roots. *Once the hair shaft has emerged from the follicle*—that is, has become visible on the scalp—*it cannot be improved, although it can be damaged.*

Rubbing it in

There is, however, one aspect of applying things to the hair and scalp which is far more important than generally recognised. It accounts for the success of many proprietary substances for hair-treatment, and it is by no means the small incidental it may seem to be; it should be emphasised, not overlooked. It is this: anything which encourages a better circulation to the scalp and which activates the hair roots tends to make for sturdier stalks and so improves the hair growth. For the cynic, there is a rich field for study in the printed instructions which accompany the bottles of hair tonics and hair foods. The bit that really counts is the rubbing, the brushing, the hair drill, the inadvertent tugging and the massage of the scalp. From any or all of these, benefit may be expected. It is no exaggeration that, in most cases, the treatment would be *even more beneficial if the preparation itself were omitted*.

The snag, of course, is that most people will not take the trouble to massage the scalp or exercise the hair unless they can "rub something in" at the same time. To this extent—and only to this extent —the money spent on preparations for encouraging hair growth may be excusable. On this point, a friend observed: "The advertisements don't agree with you. They all speak very highly of medicaments". He can have his fun; but unfortunately not all readers of advertisements are blessed with such perspicacity.

General Health

A horse which goes sick loses its fine, glossy coat of hair with astonishing rapidity. For many people, a less striking but more frequently observed instance is the domestic dog. The more dull and spiritless the coat of the animal, the more is one justified in suspecting that its health is not satisfactory. Even if not entirely reliable, it is a pretty fair guide and it also gives a clue to another factor of importance in the condition of human hair.

In humans, as in animals, the vigour of hair growth depends upon the quality and quantity of blood reaching the hair follicles. In a few cases, there may be a hereditary tendency to restricted circulation in the scalp, and this may be a serious handicap which no known treatment can remove. However, it is possible to compensate to a considerable degree, and the way the hair and scalp are handled in youth can be of immense importance. If, during childhood, the hair was vigorously and regularly brushed, and not over-protected or immobilised with close-fitting caps or hats, there is a good chance that the scalp will be thick and comparatively well supplied with blood vessels.

The more energetically the follicles can be encouraged to produce hair early in life, the greater the reserves in later years; so that the individual may expect freedom from poor hair-health, and reasonably sustained nourishment and growth.

Depth

So far as the scalp itself is concerned, there are three essentials for vigorous and healthy hair growth. These are: (1) looseness, (2) rich vascularity (a plentiful network of blood-vessels), and (3) generous thickness. The sketches opposite are approximately to scale so far as scalp and skull thicknesses are concerned, although obviously the hair thicknesses can only be represented comparatively. The point which immediately strikes one is the depth of the scalp. This can be most easily shown by X-ray, and what this reveals is in sharp contrast with the impression one may gain from palpation with the fingers. This often suggests that the scalp is little more than paper-thin, but even the thinnest—and this usually also means the baldest—of scalps is no less thick than the sole-leather one may still see in an old-fashioned shoe-repairer's shop.

These sketches also indicate the tremendous variations found in the scalps of different people. (A) shows the thin scalp of a person who would be expected almost certainly to become bald in early adult life. (B) is the typical thickness of the majority of people around us. With such a scalp, given fair attention, the owner may expect it to remain active and to produce a good growth of hair throughout his natural life. (C) is a scalp of unusual thickness, and one which can be expected also to be highly vascular. Thus equipped, the owner is likely to have vigorous and heavy growth of hair throughout his life, no matter how he may neglect it, or suffer from disturbed general health.

Thickness of scalp by itself, however, does not guarantee healthy hair growth. If it contains a high proportion of connective tissue, this may reduce the

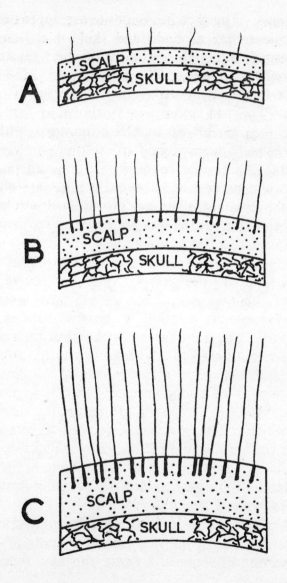

efficiency of the blood-vessels by pressing upon them and so partially closing them. Such a scalp may be recognised by its unusual firmness and immobility—it feels tight when an attempt is made to massage it. For free circulation, not only must there be a rich network of blood-vessels; these must also pass through relaxed tissues. The scalp must be loose as well as being highly vascular. Without both of these qualities, a healthy circulation is impossible; the scalp will be unable to maintain adequate nourishment to the follicles, and the hair growth will be correspondingly disappointing.

CHAPTER II

NUTRITION AND GENERAL HEALTH

Nutrition

APART from the state of the scalp itself, the vigour of hair growth is governed quite markedly by the general state of the individual's health. This, in turn, may be at the mercy of a variety of adverse circumstances. For example, today, most people are aware of the necessity for proper nutrition yet there is an increasing tendency for foodstuffs to undergo manufacturing processes. Many of these result in a lowering of the nutritional quality, so that even those who consider themselves well fed may lack proper balance in their favourite foods.

Generally, the so-called body-building and energy-producing elements in food are relatively unaffected by processing. What tend to suffer are the foods which are naturally rich in vitamins and in minerals. The manufacturers, recognising this unfortunate effect, try to make good the loss of the natural vitamins and minerals by adding to their products a variety of synthetic or "concentrate" preparations. However, although these substances may rate well in laboratory tests, it is our finding that they are not the equal of truly natural nutrients. Wherever possible, it is desirable that fresh and unprocessed foods should be used for the greater part of one's intake, and canned, frozen or otherwise preserved foodstuffs kept to a minimum. (An exception to this rule is dried food: many fruits and vegetables lend themselves well to drying, and retain a high proportion of their original goodness.) Fuller information about selection and balance of food may be found in the book *How to Eat for Health* (Thorsons).

Even if the food as eaten has been carefully selected, in some people there are digestive weaknesses which prevent its proper utilisation. In particular, it is not uncommon to find that while the foods rich in carbohydrate and protein ("energy" and "body-building") are quite well absorbed, the mineral-rich and vitamin-containing foods are poorly digested. This is understandable since these last require considerably more active digestion, and any weakness or deficiency in the stomach or intestines means that very little use is made of, for example, root and green leafy vegetables, especially in salads. This, however, is a subject too extensive for more than passing mention here.

Hindrances

Although not usually regarded as nutritional considerations, two further points must be mentioned under this heading. The first is the over-consumption of liquids, and in particular of tea or coffee. Both of these beverages have a drug content, and in unfortunate cases they can seriously disturb both digestive and circulatory efficiency. Secondly, tobacco-smoking has, as most people recognise, a marked effect on the appetite. This corresponds with a reduced capacity for digestion, with resultant poor utilisation of foods. Less generally known is the powerful adverse effect which tobacco has upon the circulation. It produces a constriction of the smallest blood-vessels, and especially those near the surface of the body and distant from the heart. The significance of this in cases of poor circulation in the scalp is too obvious to require elaboration.

Before leaving the topic of general health, two other aspects of present-day life must be mentioned. The first of these is nervous tension—whether due to conflict or to anxiety—which almost always reflects in the muscles of the neck. Tense muscles here can form a considerable barrier to the blood-circulation supplying the scalp, and anything which eases the tensions—such as massage or exercises—will minimise the obstruction. The other, often closely-associated, condition is strain in the same area due to occupational posture. Whether it be over a bench, desk or table, many people spend a considerable part of their working day bent forward. The *back* of the neck is the more important so far as circulation to the scalp is concerned, and it is here that the constant muscular tension occurs. Remembering to straighten up often, and trying to avoid more forward bending than is absolutely essential, should reduce any trouble due to this factor. Upright posture and avoidance of rigidity may improve the nutrition of the scalp more than any other treatment.

Cause and Effect

In certain long-standing or particularly severe conditions of ill-health the hair may be a sensitive indicator of the general state. It almost acts as a barometer, as for example in the dramatic response to violent fever such as typhoid. Within a short time of the fever developing, all the hair falls out; and as long as the toxic condition persists, the patient remains bald. But no local treatment for baldness is necessary. There is no call for "scalp foods" or "hair restorers". As the patient recovers, and the condition of his bloodstream returns to normal, the hair once more begins to grow. Without any special attention, the hair is restored together with returning health. Although this example is unusually clear-cut, its implications are just as true in more everyday conditions. The best all-round answer to problems of hair deficiency or disorder is to look to the general health; the hair will look after itself.

Many people are over-concerned with local *symptoms* of generalised poor bodily health, yet they would not expect to improve the weather by altering the barometer. Many forms of treatment offered to grow hair are no less ridiculous.

Good Riddance

A point which many anxious people should understand as clearly as possible is that it is *perfectly normal for the hair to fall out*. After a time, each individual hair ceases to grow. The lowest part of the follicle, in which the hair is formed, becomes inactive. No new growth is added to the hair "root", which dries, shrinks and so allows the hair to fall out.

However, while this atrophy (wasting) of the original hair-forming structure is taking place, a new follicle is forming alongside or beneath it, and from this a new, downy hair begins to be produced. Gradually, the old follicle shrivels aside, and the new one develops progressively until it takes over both the situation and the function of the old. The new hair becomes thicker as its follicle assumes full size, with vigorous new cells taking over the duty of the tired old ones.

In many mammals, this process occurs at set times —such as twice in the course of a year—and "moulting" is recognised as a perfectly natural and healthy process. In humans, there is no set time for the shedding of old hairs. But although the details differ, the healthy human is like the healthy animal in that the replacement of hair goes on year after year. It is inevitable that for each individual hair there must come a time for it to fall out. Any attempt to avoid disturbing the old, dead hair roots is bound to disappoint. Anything applied to hold the hair against the scalp only interferes with the development of the new follicle, and can only post-pone the falling of the hair by a very short time. By contrast, the more rapidly the old hairs are removed, the more opportunity is there for vigorous new hairs to grow from healthy new "roots".

Therefore no attempt should be made to conserve dead hairs. With brush and courage in both hands, they should be cleared out ruthlessly, so that future growth is not either held up or adversely affected. When an exceptional number of hairs appear to be loosening their grip, a useful routine is to massage the scalp, brush vigorously and even tug the hairs—not too violently—to clear them out. They should not be allowed to obstruct the normal outlet for the new growth.

Baldness and Intellect

It is sometimes claimed that baldness is more likely to occur in those who think deeply. In support of this contention, the analogy is offered that grass does not grow on a busy street, but this is a hopeless over-simplification. (In passing, the analogy fails because the alleged extra-heavy traffic is inside the skull, not on the outside.) The first essential in the constructive treatment of all hair troubles—singly or in combination—is that the scalp must be kept loose. This enables the local circulation to be as free, vigorous and healthy as possible.

Some of the ways in which this circulation may be impeded are quite obvious. Even a tightly-fitting hat may exert sufficient pressure to cause trouble with a thin scalp. (In understanding how markedly any continuous pressure on the surface may disturb the access of blood, it is instructive to press—quite gently—with a fingertip of one hand against the thumb nail of the other. The normal pink colouration of the nail immediately gives way to a blanched appearance, which remains as long as the pressure is applied. The colour is due to red blood, and its absence indicates the complete arrest of circulation just under the nail.)

Rapid deterioration in the quality of the hair, and eventual baldness, have been observed to occur as a direct result of regularly-worn tight or heavy headgear. Such interference, however, is unlikely to affect the deeper circulation to the head: the brain is not starved, but the scalp suffers.

The Neck

Much more serious are the less obvious factors, such as the persistent tension in muscles of the upper neck—already mentioned. Even deeper, there may be displacements of the bones of the neck which cause more complex disturbances. These conditions are known as "cervical lesions" by those trained to recognise and correct them by manipulation. Whether superficial and capable of improvement by simple personal effort, or deep and requiring skilled adjustment at another's hands, such a situation cannot be lastingly improved by any method which ignores and fails to correct the abnormality.

No matter how persuasive the salesman, or how elaborate the application, the fact remains that a scalp impoverished by obstructions in the neck is unlikely to produce a healthy growth of hair by any local treatment.

For the body, the problem is also complicated. Any deficiency in the blood circulation to the head must immediately involve a scale of vital priorities. The two structures we are concerned with at the moment are the scalp and the brain, and the body has to decide how to apportion the limited supply. A "functional compromise" has to be arrived at, and clearly the brain must have a clear preference over the scalp. One would therefore expect that the supply of blood to the brain would be maintained at the cost of that to the scalp. That reasoning applies, however, only when the entire blood supply to the head is restricted, and to the extent that immediate nourishment of the brain is of more importance than protecting it from thermal or mechanical shocks by maintaining healthy scalp and hair.

Within these limits, then, there may be a fragment of truth in the proposition that it is the intellectual or mentally-alert man who is bald. But it is a poor rule which does not work both ways, and it may not be too uncharitable to mention that most of us know men whose brains give no sign of exceptional activity, yet who possess well-polished domes.

Restoring the Balance

Assuming that there is no serious lesion—no anatomical derangement—in the structures of the neck, a deficient scalp circulation may usually be improved by a simple combination of daily routines. The first, and that which can be put into effect many times during the waking hours, is neck exercise. This need not be in any way elaborate, and an easy set consists of bending, then turning, the head slowly but strongly in each direction. Each movement may be repeated from three to a dozen times, depending on the time available and the severity of any feeling of tension before starting. It is worth emphasising that the benefit of such movements comes mainly from the strong pull which operates at either end of the range of each, and hardly at all from the large, free action in between.

For the scalp itself, it is excellent to start off the day with a cold dip for the head. Depending upon the air temperature and individual tolerance, the top of the head should be immersed in a basin of cold water for from 10 seconds to about a minute. The head should then be dried, and the hair pulled gently by running the fingers through it. (Too long an immersion in cold water will produce no better effect. The aim should be to get a vigorous response, in the form of a warm glow in the scalp as it is dried and the hair activated.) Those who have no hair on the top of the head can still apply this treatment by giving their attention to the hair around the sides, and massaging the top.

Wrinkles

In dealing with bald areas, the finger-tips should be worked *into* the scalp rather than over it—that is, carrying the skin with them and not sliding over it— so that wrinkles form between the fingers. This should be performed in a progression of movements, working first from side to side and then from front to back. If this wrinkling is done vigorously all over the scalp, it can be made to increase the local circulation to an astonishing degree, and thereby encourage permanent improvement in the strength of the hair roots. (See back flap of jacket.)

For later in the day, an evening shampoo two or three times per week may be applied. That is, using warm water, and not too much soap, the scalp should be well rubbed and then rinsed with cold water. Dried with a towel, the hair should then be pulled with the fingers and the scalp massaged until it becomes warm and suffused with freely-circulating blood.

For an overnight application the scalp compress can be effective as well as being unexpectedly soothing. The essential point about a compress is that although it is cold when applied it rapidly becomes *and stays* warm. This is in clear contrast with hot packs or fomentations, which become cool, and leave a sensation of chill afterwards. For details of the scalp compress, see page 73.

Water and Hair

Of the many widespread fallacies regarding hair health, none is more irrational than the belief that water on the hair is hurtful. Aquatic mammals, such as the seal, otter and beaver, are renowned for their beautiful coats, while among land mammals exposure to rain appears to encourage a more luxurious growth of fur. However, this may carry little weight among those concerned principally with the hair growths upon their own scalps. Many bald men are quite convinced that they should do everything possible to protect their crowns against wet. Yet among them are many who have a strong growth of beard upon their faces which are washed regularly. Not only so, they increase the access of moisture to the hairs by using shaving soaps and creams.

The unwashed portion of the scalp is completely denuded of hair, while the areas regularly washed and wetted show healthy hair growth; yet these men stick firmly to their obsession. "Greater trust hath no man than this: that his faith is maintained even at the sacrifice of his hair." It seems likely that the superstition is kept alive by the constantly recurring assertions in advertisements for hair preparations. Understandably, the manufacturers advise only their own dressings. Water, they say, is harmful to the hair, and many ingenious arguments are put forward to support this parrot-cry. Usually, the claim is that water "dries out" the hair, or "spoils its lustre", and yet the principal ingredient in most hair dressings is water.

Activity

Whatever the other substances in the dressings may be, there is one other constant factor in those which achieve practical success. To identify this, consider the significance of the following sentences, extracted from the instructions supplied with a variety of hair preparations:—

Fom one:
"Sprinkle . . . each morning, *and brush the hair thoroughly* after application."

From another:
". . . the *fingers should be moved through the hair* . . . pressing it down *in a kneading manner*."

From another:
"Apply freely, and *brush the scalp until a warm glow* is produced . . . *once or twice a day*."

From another:
"*Apply it briskly* . . . *thoroughly wet all the hair* every morning."

And another:
". . . *rubbing into the scalp* for two or three minutes, and *finally brush the hair*."

It is more than likely that the passages which we have italicised contain everything of value that the proprietors have to sell. If the same advice were carefully followed, but using plain water instead of any of the preparations, at least equally good results could be expected.

For those not yet confident enough to make this daring experiment, the following points may provide some additional assurance:—

1. While certain commercial preparations may be no more harmful than water, not one of them is capable of doing any more good.

2. Some preparations are chemically active, and may affect the general health adversely. Others immobilise the hairs and so produce a devitalisation of the scalp.

3. A scalp which is thin, tight and with a poor circulation of blood is incapable of producing healthy hair growth. The advice given with the "tonics" and "hair foods", to brush vigorously and to rub the preparation well in, may do much to loosen a tight scalp and so improve the local circulation.

Best Results

The user of any hair tonic or preparation (no matter what its name or composition) who wishes to obtain the very best possible results is advised to observe the following simple instructions, if results have not so far been entirely satisfactory:—

(*a*) First, damp the hair and scalp with cold water.

*(*b*) Apply the preparation according to the directions on the package or bottle.

(*c*) Massage and knead the scalp, and pull the hair, as suggested in previous pages.

(*d*) Repeat three to four times daily.

One patient of ours was a regular client of a well-known London hair stylist, and after one of her visits she wrote to us: "Yesterday, I went to ————'s and I noticed that the assisant who used to treat me has the condition which used to trouble me. He had it beautifully camouflaged, of course, but I told him how I had cured myself with your methods. He was very sceptical to begin with, especially about the free use of water and compresses. But then I told him about Mrs ————'s case, and this seemed to convince him. He asked me innumerable questions, especially about pulling the hair, and said he would give it a trial". In itself, this little aside proves nothing—it might only indicate that a good professional knows when to humour his customers!—but at least one lady had the courage of her own experience.

---

* Better results are to be anticipated if (b) is omitted.

CHAPTER III

COMMON DISORDERS OF HAIR AND SCALP

Alopecia

ONE of the most distressing forms of scalp disorder is *alopecia*. In this, the hair loses its normal vigour and elasticity, becoming thin and brittle, then falls out over an area of the scalp. Home treatment can be of great benefit, if carried out along the correct lines, and persevered with conscientiously. Usually, the trouble first becomes noticeable with the appearance of bald patches gradually developing on the scalp.

In order to understand what is happening, and how to deal with it, a little must be known about the normal processes of the growth and shedding of hair. Each individual hair has a rate of growth, a period of life and a typical length depending on the region of the body in which it is situated. The lifetime of a particular hair on the scalp is normally in the range of from two to six years, at the end of which period it is normally replaced by a new hair, in the way already outlined. In each case, the characteristic lifetime is consistent with the type of hair, and should there by any shortening of the interval in the case of scalp hair there must follow a tendency to baldness.

In the first stage, there is a preponderance of short-lived hairs, and this passes to the stage in which the hair length is diminished: each hair falling out before it has attained its characteristic length. There are other factors involved in *alopecia*, but the patient —always an adult—first notices a slight thinning of the hair. As the years pass, the thinning is progressive until the typical signs of baldness appear, usually showing first at the vertex—the crown— and as a receding hairline above the forehead.

Early Signs

It is easy to be introspective and over-anxious about the state of one's hair, even to the extent of imagining the rapid arrival of a deficiency which has in fact existed for years. It is a characteristic of many people that their minds go from one extreme to the other when they consider their own physical condition. They either believe themselves to be perfectly well or to be seriously ill. So far as their hair is concerned, they can see no condition in between being "normal" and "going bald", although there are in reality many stages in deterioration. It is therefore not with the intention of encouraging intensive self-analysis, but rather of giving as much reassurance as possible, that the following points are raised. The earlier any condition of degeneration is recognised, the more effective can be remedial treatment.

If the hairs which come out each day—in brush or comb—are carefully examined, it will be found that there are two kinds; some are the same thickness right up to the end, which has obviously been cut; others taper to fine, silky points. The cut-ended hairs may be of any length without significance—since the main factor is the hair style adopted by the individual. But the tapering hairs should be long, and normally occur in the combings only of those who allow their hair to grow to at least many inches in length. Their presence in the combings of those who have their hair cut short is not a good sign. Short, pointed hairs, easily detached from the scalp, are hairs which have not lived out their full lives. The roots have died before the stalks attained sufficient length to be cut by the scissors. (In passing, it should be noted that although we talk of hairs "living a full life", this does not imply that the hair which shows above the scalp is alive. What we mean is that the region of the hair follicle which actually produces hair substance remains active for something like the two to six years already mentioned.)

Stages

The proportion of short, tapering hairs is a fairly reliable indication of the extent to which alopecia has developed. As time passes, the tendency is for each new hair to live a shorter life than its predecessor. With this, a higher proportion of immature hairs appear in the combings, and at the same time many hairs never reach full thickness. They revert to the appearance of lanugo, and this process goes on until all the healthy hair is replaced by this fine, downy growth. This marks the completion of the first stage of baldness. But *so long as these fine hairs are still visible*, it is not impossible to re-attain a healthy growth of hair. On the other hand, if nothing is done to improve the general health, the tone of the scalp and the local circulation, even this lanugo may disappear, leaving the scalp truly bald, shining and perfectly smooth. Once this stage is reached, there is no known way of regaining a normal growth of hair. The follicles, or bulbs, from which the lanugo springs may be shrivelled and starved, but they are still hair bulbs. When the lanugo disappears, the follicles will have been reabsorbed—reverted to the simple skin structure from which they were originally developed. In one respect the hair is like a daffodil—without a bulb it cannot grow.

Dandruff and Heredity

A common accompaniment of the early stage of alopecia is the presence of many small, browny-white scales. These increase in number as the loss of hair progresses, and are often obvious as an untidy scattering on the shoulders of clothing. Those who like impressive names may call the condition *furfuraceous desquamation* or *pityriasis*. Popularly, it is known as dandruff—an adequate name for our purpose. The only discomfort among its symptoms are a characteristic ticklish or mildly itchy sensation in the scalp, and a slight feeling of unpleasant warmth or even of heat.

The scales of dandruff are produced by the surface of the skin—the epithelium—and indicate a significant deviation from the normal state of its condition. Dandruff, and its accompanying symptoms, are seldom found in any serious degree among women, whereas the man whose father was bald is more than likely to follow his example. There appears to be a distinct hereditary factor in dandruff and baldness. Although not in itself a vital disorder, dandruff is frequently associated with quite serious conditions. For example, it often appears after the individual has undergone medication for skin diseases, urogenital infections or persistent fevers. (That is, after what we regard as *suppressive*—as distinct from corrective—treatment.) Dandruff is also often associated with long-standing emotional or nervous strains and conflicts—which are also capable of over-taxing the vitality and, by a complex series of events, ultimately leading to baldness.

We have already noted that unhealthy hair is less durable and less elastic than hair of normal health, and there are corresponding changes in the scalp itself. This becomes devitalised as the active, functional cells are replaced by inert connective tissue. In the later stages of dandruff, this invasion has developed to a serious extent, with a massive and dense meshwork of fibrous tissue. This prevents the microscopic muscles of the follicles from acting freely, and obstructs the flow of blood by pressing upon the blood-vessels. The shrinking and thinning of the scalp is progressive, and the resultant inactivity and diminished blood supply are the major factors in causing wasting and starvation of the follicles, which are ultimately obliterated.

Microscopic

The mechanism of dandruff may be better understood if a typical scale is examined under the microscope. It is seen to be made up of a large number of cells—such as normally occur on the surface of the skin—cemented together by matter with a horny and fatty character. The dandruff scale is, in fact, a modification of the normal process whereby the skin renovates itself. In health, the scalp keeps itself clean and wholesome by constantly shedding its flattened, microscopically small, dead surface cells. Since these are thrown off individually, they are quite imperceptible to ordinary inspection. Yet, despite its reduced vital activity, the scalp with dandruff is the one which appears to be the more active. This is so because the far greater number of normal cells—in healthy scalp function—are just too small to be seen. The same process is, of course, occurring at all times over the entire skin of the body, and it accounts for the seeming paradox that the skin can often be kept cleaner and sweeter with simple rubbing than by applications of soap and water. Exposure of the skin to fresh air and friction is unequalled for producing a clear and wholesome complexion, and the same principle applies to the scalp.

Secretions

The presence of clumped, dead cells is the characteristic of dandruff, and the important question is what makes them so form. The essential factor is the abnormally gummy nature of the scalp secretions, which bind the cells into visible scales. The secretions should normally serve to coat the hair with an oily film of sebum (a soft grease quite similar to the lanolin of sheep's wool). In dandruff, there is a change in the nature of the secretion, just as in catarrh there is a change in the nature of the mucus which is normally secreted to protect the linings of nose and throat. Dandruff, which is the visible evidence of abnormal secretion in the scalp, precedes and accompanies baldness in the same way that a discharge from the nose and throat (which may become dried and gummy) accompanies catarrh.

But, and this most important to understand, *dandruff is not the cause of baldness*, any more than a nasal discharge is the *cause* of catarrh; it is a *symptom* of disorder. In both dandruff and catarrh, the exuded matter is unpleasant and of a strongly adherent nature. In both cases it appears to us to be material better thrown outside the body than allowed to remain circulating in the blood. In both dandruff and catarrh, we believe that the living tissues concerned are making desperate efforts to help cleanse the body fluids of an excessive accumulation of wastes. This can be described as an accessory form of elimination—supplementing the normal functions of skin, kidneys, lungs and liver— and we believe that it can often be life-saving. That is, when the processes are understood, and allowed to run their proper course, there is an overall gain in wholesomeness.

Suppression

But if the original causes of excess waste in the system are not removed, and particularly if the extra eliminative effort is discouraged by medication or other suppressive treatment, the accumulating and driven-back toxic materials may cause serious vital damage. In the case of dandruff, it may be quite possible to prevent its formation by some kind of chemical substance applied to the scalp. But to the extent that the treatment succeeds in its aim, the local distress—the build-up of wastes in and around the hair roots and glands—is intensified. By treating dandruff in this way, the development of baldness may be much accelerated. To the existing condition, of poor circulation and accumulated wastes in the cells of the follicles, is added the depressant effect of the medicament. Only to a mind capable of seeing dandruff and baldness as totally unrelated diseases can such treatment seem justifiable. (There is a seemingly logical argument which says that dandruff usually leads to baldness, therefore if dandruff is stopped baldness will not develop. The answer to that is implicit in the foregoing paragraph.) We would rather say that dandruff is an indication of an attempt within the scalp to avoid further degeneration; that therefore nothing should be done to interfere with its expression, but that everything possible should be done to improve the basic condition. Dandruff should not be "cured", any more than a fire alarm should be muffled. Both are urgent calls for rescue operations.

Alopecia Areata

The ordinary type of *alopecia*, which we have discussed up to now, is in no way characterised by dramatic appearance or development. In striking contrast, *alopecia areata* can be both sudden and spectacular. Its outstanding feature is its fairly rapid onset, in the form of a roundish, sharply-defined bald patch. This may spread slowly, or two or three separate patches may run together to form a large irregular area. In the most severe cases, the process may continue so that not only does the entire scalp lose its hair, but that of the entire body also disappears. In typical cases, the appearance of the skin itself is not changed, and in the milder forms of the condition there may be only one—or perhaps two—small patches on the scalp or in the beard.

These gradually produce hair again, and without any sign of related developments. This is described as *benign alopecia areata*.

In contrast with the form previously discussed, *alopecia areata* occurs mainly among comparatively young people, and both sexes are similarly liable to be affected. Preceding symptoms are uncommon, although occasionally there may have been a history of headache, or of itching, tingling and abnormal warmth in the scalp. The dramatic element may be introduced by the falling out of a whole bunch of hair while it is being brushed or combed, and quite without any prior indication or discomfort. Even more alarming, the clump of hair may be found on the pillow in the morning.

Appearance

The affected patch of scalp is usually quite bald, but occasionally a few perfectly healthy hairs are found in scattered isolation upon it. If examined immediately after its appearance, the skin in the affected area is found to be slightly raised—that is, thicker than the normal skin adjacent to it. Gradually, it resumes its former depth and hair growth begins spontaneously, as already noted. In some cases, one patch recovers and another just as suddenly develops in another part of the scalp.

The immediate cause of *alopecia areata* is a matter of varying opinion, and the favoured explanation in orthodox circles is the presence of a vegetable parasite. Difficulty in accepting this as a complete account is due partly to the different organisms claimed as responsible by various investigators. There seems to be no agreement except on the most general terms. Also, and this is much more telling in practice, antiseptic or bactericidal applications have no beneficial effect on the course of the condition. We would say that the presence of a germ, and its precise identification, are matters of little moment. What does seem much more significant is the nervous basis of the condition. This is confirmed when, as is not uncommon, the nerve supply to a particular part of the scalp is injured and the hair growth suffers in a fashion very similar to that of *alopecia areata*. A second indication of nervous involvement is the fact that the skin over an alopecia patch is always very pale. To the trained observer, this indicates a disturbance of the vaso-motor mechanism (nervous control) of the blood vessels.

Simple Cases

Although any nerve disorder is likely to be associated with a broader and deeper disharmony, and may lead to more complex conditions, the treatment in any recent case of *alopecia areata* is simple and effective. The scalp should be rubbed and massaged vigorously—to assist circulation and hence to ensure the best possible conditions for restoration of normal function—and frequently. Also, and this is of considerable importance, the scalp should be kept really clean. And not with shampoos of doubtful detergent content, but with a minimum of mild soap and a maximum of vigorously-applied water. Encouragement of the circulation and cleanliness provide all that is required in the way of local applications for a rapid and uncomplicated recovery. In most cases, this should be complete in a month or two. Occasionally, there are recurrences, and if nothing is done to improve the general health—or an unsatisfactory condition of the scalp itself—the disorder may continue to embarrass for many years.

Long-Standing Cases

If *alopecia areata* has existed for a long period, simple home treatment is unlikely to be sufficient. The patient should consult a Registered Naturopath who will be able to check a number of important possible factors. For example, there may be some form of injury or strain (lesion) in the neck region of the spine. A nerve trunk may be affected here, on its way to the scalp, and so produce a persistently disturbed nutrition there. Skilled manipulation and instruction in corrective exercise may produce a remarkable improvement in such cases. As a further complication, the composition of the patient's bloodstream may be abnormal, so that dietary habits and other daily routines may have to be carefully adjusted. It should be obvious that where factors of this kind are involved, properly-trained attention is essential. Also that no hair tonic or alleged hair food can offer more than marginal assistance, even when perfectly honest advice about scalp-massage and brushing are thrown in as a makeweight.

Seborrhoea

The normal functioning of the sebaceous glands produces enough greasy material to coat the hair shafts, making them more effectively water-repellent and at the same time giving an improved appearance of glossiness. One way in which this secretion may be disturbed has already been outlined in the discussion of dandruff—it becomes hardened and gummy. Another, equally unpleasant, disorder is an excessive flow, known as *seborrhoea*. In the scalp, this causes the hair to become oily and limp in appearance, and greasy to the touch. Quite commonly, the nose and forehead are affected together with the scalp, and in severe cases the skin looks as if it were ingrained with oily dust and dirt.

The background of *seborrhoea* is often a disturbed balance of blood constituents, such as occurs in simple anaemia, or chlorosis. The causes of this are frequently a combination of the intense physiological activities of adolescence and an unsatisfactory nutrition. *Seborrhoea* occurs most commonly at puberty and in early adult life, and if there are no accompanying indications of unsatisfactory general health, the local treatments already described for toning up the scalp are usually sufficient. However, it is more than likely that nutritional guidance is called for, and any sign of bloodlessness confirms the need for professional advice, from a registered Naturopath.

Splitting

A common, and comparatively minor, sign of disorder in the hair is splitting at the ends. It occurs most usually in long hair, and is thus seen mainly in women, or in men with full beards. It is quite possible for every single hair to be split in this way, although it may call for really close examination to detect this. In Latin, the name of the condition is *scissura pilorum*, and this term is used to impress an anxious client with the seriousness of his plight. Both in advertising and by word of mouth the suggestion is made that splitting hairs are a danger sign, calling for immediate treatment of the hair.

This attitude is close to the outmoded nonsense of singeing the hair after cutting "to seal the ends". (Sometimes this is claimed to prevent the access of infection from without; sometimes to prevent the escape of "sap" or "energy" from the hair-shaft. All such ideas are based on ignorance and imagination.) Splitting seems to indicate nothing more significant than that the hair was produced under less than ideal conditions. There seems to be a link with finger- and toe-nails, which are in many people found to have deep ridges or corrugations running along them. Hair and nail are closely allied, both in their composition and in their method of production from specialised skin cells. If these cells are in any way under strain, or imperfectly nourished by the general bloodstream, their products are in turn liable to be imperfect. Ridged nails are often associated with overworked kidneys, and these organs are much less often in any way diseased than merely suffering from thoughtless or misinformed habits of the individual. Among these, the commonest are the liberal use of tea or coffee, and the drinking of much water. (The last often being done against all one's instincts, in the fallacious belief that it "helps to flush out the kidneys". It would be true to say that copious drinking tends tends to flush *away* the kidneys!)

However, for the moment it is enough to note that splitting of hair ends is in no way serious in itself.

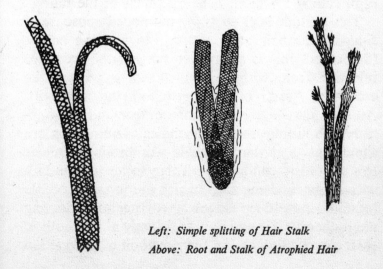

Left: Simple splitting of Hair Stalk
Above: Root and Stalk of Atrophied Hair

CHAPTER IV

SOME RARER DISORDERS: PERSEVERANCE

Atrophy

THE splitting described previously is limited strictly to the extreme ends of the hairs. In quite a different category is splitting throughout the length of the shaft. This is associated in some cases with atrophy (wasting) of the hair, otherwise known as *atrophia pilorum propria*, although simpler conditions may also be responsible (see later). True atrophy is a distressing, and often disfiguring, ailment. It demands serious attention because it involves a more rapid and complete loss of hair growth than any other condition. (*Alopecia areata* may show up more dramatically, but with every prospect of fairly steady recovery.) In atrophy, the hairs become rough, dry, lustreless and brittle, and give the general appearance of being "dead". There is often a teasing out of the hair shaft into microscopic strands, which makes it look swollen and disfiguring.

The splitting which occurs in the hair shaft is usually into three or four segments—rather than the division into two which occurs in much less serious conditions—and each segment in turn may be broken down. Another feature of the condition is the presence of hairs much more slender than their

51

neighbours. If one of these too-thin hairs is pulled out, the bulb at its end will be found to be small and shrivelled when examined under strong magnification. The splitting occurs within the hair follicle, with the hair substance being produced by the various parts of the follicle failing to unite normally. There is at the same time a deficiency of the substance so that a ragged and irregular mass is formed instead of a uniform and firmly constructed column. Although not visible on ordinary examination, the split shaft starts out from an undersized bulb, from which it emerges looking rather like the rounded ends of a couple of hairpins.

Exposed to normal wear and tear, the atrophying hair has insufficient elasticity and toughness, so that it breaks and splinters to give the unhappy appearance already described.

Very little can be expected from any local treatment of true atrophy, since its causes lie deep within the individual's general condition. This obviously cannot be more than mentioned at this time, and professional advice will almost certainly be necessary to suggest or provide constitutional treatment towards the improvement of general health.

Fevers

The simpler condition, which has some signs similar to those of true atrophy, occurs after severe and prolonged fevers—or any other comparable disorder affecting the system as a whole. Although the fever itself is often held to be responsible for disrupting the hair growth, there is reason for suspecting that in many cases a much more serious factor is the drugging which has been administered as treatment for the fever. Many modern pharmaceuticals have much more powerful effects than their forerunners, and their side-effects are correspondingly violent.

In such comparatively short-term disorders, the effect on the hair is usually less catastrophic than in true atrophy. The hair becomes dull, lustreless and dry, having little tensile strength or elasticity. It splits readily and breaks with sharp bending or comparatively slight tugging.

Here again, it will be obvious that local treatment is of comparatively little value by itself, and must take second place to a generalised improvement in the individual's health. However, with the passing of the fever or other distress, and discontinuation of medication, the system should gradually return to normal, and hair growth follows suit.

Ringworm

In young people, there occurs a disorder of the scalp which is easily confused with *alopecia areata*—previously described—and which is not altogether amenable to home treatment. This is ringworm of the scalp. It is not found in the adult, and almost always occurs before the age of puberty. In contrast with *alopecia areata*, the hair loss is gradual, and the affected area does not become completely bald. The hair follicles protrude, with the appearance of goose-flesh, and around the borders of the patch are broken-off hairs. Within the patch, the skin is usually scaly and the hairs upon it may be easily pulled out. Microscopic examination shows the presence of parasitic organisms—most often fungal. In some cases, the patch looks like an abscess; it is severely inflamed, and the presence of the typical fungi (consisting of tiny, round shining bodies and red structures—*mycelia*) may be the only sure diagnosis of the condition.

Differences

Children with this trouble are frequently treated for long periods for *alopecia areata*, although there need be no confusion. The rule is that *alopecia areata* develops after puberty; the area involved is entirely bald; the hair loss is usually complete; the hair follicles do not protrude—instead they may be completely obliterated; the area of the loss is clean-cut and has no broken-off hairs; the surface is smooth and healthy in appearance and there is no scaly matter. Further, the hairs around the border of the patch are firmly anchored.

Care

In ringworm, constitutional treatment may have to be extensive, to ensure the return of normal and vigorous health. Individual towels, comb, brush and soap should be the rule, and under no circumstances should the patient use such articles belonging to another person. The hair should be kept cut short, and hair and scalp should be frequently and thoroughly cleansed. Hairs which detach easily should be removed from the patch once or twice daily, followed by a soapy rinse using a mild soap, preferably free from scent or dye. There is no better way of cleansing scales and other debris from the surface without injury. Burning with X-ray is sometimes suggested, but this is destructive and suppressive, meaning that serious complications are likely to follow, even many years afterwards. To accept such treatment is to imperil the child's future health, in return for—at best—an immediate reduction of the superficial symptoms. It should have been obvious, from the opening sentence of this paragraph, that the surface disorder is probably the least of the child's health problems; treating it alone—and by suppressive means—is to intensify the internal strains.

Neuritis

When a nerve becomes inflamed, the area of skin which it supplies is liable to become reddened, thickened and peculiarly shiny. Neuritis is therefore not only evident as a particularly unpleasant pain, but its effects can be seen in its surface distribution. When neuritis occurs in the scalp, the hair growth is also liable to be disturbed. A common effect is the loss of pigment, so that the hair grows white, or growth ceases and the hair falls out. An alternative effect is a coarsening of the hair growth, which is less noticeable on the scalp than on other parts of the body. That is, when the nerve is seriously disturbed, the follicles controlled by it may either have their functions depressed—even totally interrupted—or there may be a frenzied over-activity, encouraged by the increased temperature and blood supply of inflammation.

No local treatment is likely to improve such a condition, since the causes are systemic. The logical approach is therefore through nutrition and other forms of treatment beneficial to the entire nervous system. There may be related disorders of vital organs, and the patient should be guided by a practitioner qualified to treat the body as a whole. Although the disorder may appear to have a localised and limited incidence, it is symptomatic of a general distress and its treatment should always be on the broadest possible lines.

Perseverance

It is a general finding that any physical disorder must take an appreciable time to correct. There are cases in which seemingly miraculous disappearances of symptoms have occurred, but we have reservations about the relative significance of the physical and the emotional factors involved. Where a true physical deterioration has occurred, the recovery must take time which bears some relationship to the period of its development. In our work, we have a rule of thumb which sets this relationship at one month per year. This means that it will take at least a month of serious application to undo the effects of each year of the kind of living which produced and perpetuated the disorder. And that means under really good conditions: where many obstacles present themselves, the remedial effort may have to be considerably prolonged.

A scalp which has been tight for—say—five years, and which has begun to lose hair vigour quite noticeably, may therefore take almost six months to be brought back to a truly relaxed and well-nourished state. It will take time after that, too, before the improvement begins to be evident in the hair. There has to be a logical sequence in the progress to normality. In a real sense, most people have been producing their condition of health for most of their lives. If the condition is unsatisfactory, the recovery time usually is much longer with an elderly person than with a child.

Start Early

A *tight* scalp may be produced in a child within quite a few years if scalp and hair are neglected, and particularly if any tight or hard-rimmed headgear is worn. A *thin* scalp may be hereditary, but neglect—often accompanied by unsatisfactory nutrition and emotional environment—is often the major factor. To ensure a loose, vascular and healthy scalp later in life, it is never too early to begin with vigorous brushing of the hair, scalp massage and other attentions as described earlier.

Even when baldness is imminent, or has actually arrived, a few minutes' attention morning and evening—massage to the scalp, cold dip, vigorous brushings of the hair and pulling it through the fingers—will do much to reverse the deterioration. The really noticeable improvement must take time, but to the individual the beginnings of returning vitality should become evident within a much shorter period.

The rule of thumb quoted above is intended to give a sense of proportion to the situation. Once, a patient complained at the end of 10 days that our suggestions were a failure, because his scalp was still tight and no hair had arrived. There was a history of 60 years of neglect, and he was despairing because the deterioration had not been made good by a total of less than two hours' attention! This relationship was brought firmly to his notice and he resumed his efforts. He was able to report an encouraging response only a few weeks later.

CHAPTER V

HAIR COLOUR

Colour

THE many shades of hair colour are produced by pigment—a brownish material called *melanin*—present in varying amounts. If it is abundant, the hair is dark; if in moderate quantity the hair is brownish and if totally absent the hair is white. However, there is a further factor in the character of the *melanin* itself, and this may vary from an almost bluish tint in very black hair to a reddish colour in the deep coppery or light golden varieties. The combination of a particular density of pigment and of its characteristic tone produces the strikingly individual effect which may identify a family or a race.

The pigment is formed in the cells of the follicle, and is exactly comparable with that occurring in the other skin cells and giving the skin as a whole its characteristic colour. In passing it may be noted that strong sunlight encourages the formation of *melanin* in the skin cells. People with dark colouring tan readily, whereas those of fair colouring may produce only a few freckles. However, once the *melanin* has been deposited in the hair shaft, it tends to be bleached by strong sunlight. This accounts for the seemingly paradoxical—yet attractive—combination sometimes found of a skin which tans to a golden colour but with hair which bleaches to flaxen. The granules of *melanin* in the hair cannot be replaced once the hair is formed, whereas those in the skin can be constantly reinforced from the living layers below the surface.

Greying

Gradual greying of the hair with age is not a disorder. Fading colour is no more a disease than is the darkening which occurs in many individuals between early childhood and maturity. It is normal for the pigmentation to alter in density with age, and its reduction need not be associated with any lack of vigour in the hair growth. Even white hair should remain thick and vigorous until a really advanced age. Just when the colouring starts to fade depends upon a combination of individual factors, among which heredity is a major consideration. That is, if either parent greyed early there is a probability of it occurring in the offspring.

Sudden greying is a different matter, and one has to be careful not to misunderstand the many reports of hair turning white in 24 hours. It is inconceivable that anything other than bleaching by chemical or by light could remove the pigment from the hair above the skin. So far as anything in the way of constitutional shock is concerned, this can only affect the hair in process of being formed within the follicle. Ordinarily it must take at least a day for non-pigmented hair to become visible above the surface, and many weeks or months before the entire head of hair is replaced by the altered growth. In other words, although the hair may start quite suddenly to *grow* white, the process of *turning* white a head of hair must be a gradual one.

History records many cases of rapid change in hair colour to grey or white. Sir Thomas Moore and Marie Antoinette are celebrated instances, and a more recent example was a young naval officer who came to us with completely white hair. He told us that this was the result of falling from the mast of a sailing ship. It was a high fall, and he had time to realise that death must be inevitable. However, he cleared the bulwarks by inches and, to his total amazement, was rescued unhurt from the sea. He assured us most positively that by next morning his hair was white.

Treatment

Whether loss of colour takes place slowly or dramatically quickly, it is far less amenable to remedial treatment than conditions which involve the growth and vitality of the hair. Once again, we have to give consideration to the general health. Patients who suffer from recurrent fevers, or whose nervous state undergoes repeated and violent changes, are prone to have speckled hair. That is, the hair shafts are seen to consist of alternating lengths of pigmented and colourless tissue. The pigmented sections are the parts which were produced during the periods of normal health, whereas the un-pigmented parts were formed during the times of physical depression or nervous collapse.

This suggests, logically, that what is good for the patient's general health is probably also good for his hair colour. We have already seen that the vigour of hair growth is closely related to the state of health, and the laying down of pigment in the forming hair is one of the functions of the follicle. When the follicles receive their normal supplies of materials, through a properly balanced and well-nourished blood stream, they are enabled to produce hair which is strong, well-formed and characteristically pigmented. Disturbed nervous controls, or disordered blood chemistry, can prevent their proper function. A diet adequate in fresh and wholesome foodstuffs, plus attention to breathing and the muscles of the neck—to encourage oxygenation and to remove physical impediments to the circulation—are possibly the most immediately significant remedial measures.

Dyes

The application of dye to the hair cannot be lightly recommended. A minor, but troublesome, annoy-ance is that the dye can be applied only to that part of the hair shaft which is above the skin. Within a very few days of application, undyed hair begins to be visible close to the scalp, giving an unsightly and conspicuous white line. This calls for another application of dye, and with such frequently-repeated treatment the second—and far more serious —problem is liable to occur. This is the risk of inter-action between the chemicals of the dye and the living cells of the scalp.

The majority of dyes currently marketed have been carefully selected and tested to minimise the risk of toxic effects, but it is still unfortunately true that the dyes which produce the strongest effects—for making grey or white hair very dark or black—are also powerful in their biological effects. Applied with skill and precision, they may produce no appreciable ill-effect in the scalp; but self-applied in generous amounts—and often—the hazards are really serious.

Poisoning

In passing, it should be noted that not only are hair *dyes* to be regarded with some suspicion: so-called tonics for the hair and scalp have a bad record. Quinine is a favourite ingredient in tonics, and this drug has far deeper and more devastating effects than are generally recognised. It penetrates to the living layers of the scalp, and from there may spread into deeper structures and organs, by way of the bloodstream. It is unusual for a sufferer from giddiness and headache to connect these symptoms with the use of a hair tonic, but the link can be short and direct. Congested headache above the eyes, fullness in the head, ringing in the ears, dizziness and disturbances of vision have all been traced to drugs applied to the scalp.

In the deepest dyes, metallic salts have been used, as have the even more insidious compounds of the coal-tar group. Sometimes the poisoning effect shows quickly, and the user may thus be spared the worse effects which follow prolonged applications. In other cases, the dyes may be used for a considerable time—with no evident harm—and then quite suddenly produce a severe and persistent irritation. This possibility should be kept in mind because it is a popular fallacy that something which one has done for a long time cannot be the cause of a new ailment: on the contrary, the very length of its contact makes its responsibility the more certain.

There has been a long-overdue improvement in the marketing of preparations intended for use on the hair and scalp, and the probability is that the risks of a generation ago have diminished to insignificance. However, "trade secrets" do not always operate to the benefit of the consumer, and some of the classic hazards may still be with us. In the hope that they may be of historical importance only, here are a few typical examples: eczema and urticaria; irritation and inflammation of scalp, face or around the eyes; symptoms of poisoning by copper, lead and mercury; death from the toxic effects of paraphenylene-diamine (a coal-tar derivative).

Delayed Effects
When—as occasionally happens—a hairdresser

is taken to court by a customer who has suffered ill-effects from some applied preparation, two considerations should be borne in mind. First, the high probability that the unfortunate reaction was not produced solely by the treatment blamed for it, but by the cumulative effects of many previous treatments of a more or less similar nature. "Sensitisation" is well recognised in other fields of medicine and in industrial poisoning. Secondly, that of all the untoward effects produced by medication or chemical treatment of the hair and scalp, only a tiny proportion become public knowledge. In most cases, the apparent cause-and-effect sequence is not clean-cut enough for legal proceedings to be instituted.

Many weeks, or even months, may elapse between the application and the appearance of symptoms. And when they do manifest, it is not necessarily upon the head; it may be in or upon some distant part of the body. The average sufferer will consult his doctor, and unless he has reason to be unusually suspicious the doctor will diagnose from the appearance of the outbreak. He may call it "urticaria" or "eczema", or he may blame "a germ", and will probably prescribe a soothing ointment or antibiotic. The real culprit is either unsuspected or only vaguely wondered about.

Patience

For those who must have immediate results, dyes have the practical advantages of being quick and positive—albeit with some risk of complication. On the other hand, the fact that instant success does not follow home treatment of greyness by natural methods need not discourage the experimenter. With patience, astonishingly good results are sometimes achieved, but the prospects are reasonable only when the condition is tackled early. The treatments previously discussed for encouraging vigorous growth also favour the restoration of natural colour. But obviously it is futile to expect pigment to return to the hair once the follicles have lost their ability to extract the substances from the bloodstream and inject them into the growing hair. A brief interruption—such as by a fever or passing nervous disorder, as already mentioned—rarely destroys the mechanism of pigmentation, but a prolonged cessation leads to wasting and permanent loss of function.

Example

A case history may encourage those faced with the problem of prematurely greying hair. When first seen, the patient had what he called his "quiff"—a thin, sparse tuft of white hair which was kept carefully drawn across the top of a shiny, hard, tight dome of scalp. For years, this tuft had been gently handled, and it had slowly diminished in volume. It was a losing fight. More and more the successful business man was "coming out on top". On our advice, the scalp was massaged regularly, with gentle pulling of the hair. The patient was warned that the hair might begin to come out, but that the treatment should be continued. In a matter of a few weeks, the cherished hairs did indeed come out, to the patient's obvious distress and more than a trace of suspicion. But a few more weeks and, in place of the thin, colourless hair, there began to appear new hair, vigorous in texture *and dark in colour*. By this time, the scalp had become comparatively loose and healthy. Nor was this all: the patient had begun to hold his head high, and to walk with a more youthful and sprightly step. These effects were probably more psychological than physical—even though an improved posture can lead to benefits in all systems of the body—but there was no denying the apparent renewal of youth . . . and a man is as old as he feels.

Simple Measures—
Outdoor activity—such as brisk walking—plus a daily cold water splash and a scalp bath three or four times a day; vigorous massage of the scalp, combing, brushing and pulling the hair; a daily—or in summer twice-daily—vegetable salad and a nightly scalp compress will do much to encourage a return of natural colouring. These simple measures have often succeeded when other methods have failed.

CHAPTER VI

A MESSAGE OF HOPE

Day by Day

SUNLIGHT—whether natural or from a sun-lamp—can be beneficial to the skin and to the hair growing from it. Scalp massage, neck exercises, the use of water compresses to scalp and neck, gentle to vigorous brushing and pulling of the hair—all these are excellent ways of encouraging vigorous hair growth. Above all, simple soap-and-water cleanliness will avoid any risk of the more unpleasant forms of scalp disorder. Even the much-feared ringworm, which can spread alarmingly among school children, never becomes established in those children whose hair and scalp are kept clean *and whose general nutrition is satisfactory.* The general health is paramount, and no local treatment is likely to have a satisfactory effect, in established disorders of the scalp, if the patient's health is much below par.

Caution

In his desire to improve his condition, the reader should keep firmly in mind the absolute necessity for self-effort. Many advertisements seem to offer easy methods and to promise alluring results, but it is seldom that real health results from such treatments. Bodily health, like hair health, does not come in bottles. It results from a persevering adherence to sensible ways of living. Wonderful claims are made for new drugs, biological preparations and even for operations. In our technological age, such methods are described as "scientific", whereas the search for underlying causes of disorder and the attempt to understand and take remedial action is regarded as unscientific! The rational approach calls for courage as well as for understanding; just as dead hairs may have to be pulled out to make way for new, living hair, so the comforting process of symptom-suppression has to be ruthlessly discarded.

In scalp conditions, symptomatic treatment must in the long run fail miserably—as it does in other bodily disorders. There is no substitute for the removal of the causes of the ailment. That must forever remain in the basis of real cure. With symptom-treatment, complications multiply rapidly. The *harmless* medications, the *painless* operations and the *simple* but miraculous injections of today are the foundations of tomorrow's chronic diseases. Every honest observer is alarmed not only by the great increase in suffering, but by the growing death rate from heart disease, diabetes, asthma, arthritis, kidney disease and cancer. There must be a cause for these results, and we are not alone in believing that the more powerful—the more "miraculous"—the medication used to treat simple disorders, the more agonising and shattering the breakdown which must ensue.

Wholesomeness

Sir William Arbuthnot Lane once said: "If these diseases are peculiar to civilisation, and never affect healthy tissues, it is obvious that the only way of avoiding them is by keeping the body in a state of health. No other way has ever been suggested". Immunisation is not the answer, as any informed epidemiologist can readily confirm. In the worst epidemics, immunisation is powerless and only a genuine improvement in the general hygiene brings relief. Wholesome nutrition and simple cleanliness are absolute essentials, and if either is seriously deficient no kind of medication, vaccination or injection can protect the individual.

The foregoing paragraphs may appear somewhat intense to the reader who is concerned only with a comparatively mild disorder of the scalp, but the principle is consistent in all cases of physical ailment —only the degree of its urgency varies. It is *not* absolutely safe to use a "mild" antiseptic lotion or shampoo on the scalp. It is far more perilous to apply a deadly poison in the attempt to kill off a suspected infestation by fungus. These chemicals may produce a temporary cessation of the symptom, but the true cost is infinitely higher than the cash price of the preparations. It is the vitality of the living tissues which is spent, and once that is gone it can never be restored.

There is no substitute for self-effort if true, lasting cure is the goal.

Hope

The suggestions given throughout this book will lead to the promotion of vigorous hair growth, unless atrophy (wasting) of the follicles (hair roots) is so far advanced that recovery is impossible. In the comparatively rare case in which the follicles have been completely destroyed, there is no known means of producing hair growth.

If bodily vigour can be regained before too long a period of inertia has elapsed, it is probable that strong and healthy hair can be grown once again. If you are successful, do not keep your achievement a secret: pass along the good news that health—and this includes hair health—is not produced by medication, surgery or proprietary preparations. It is the logical outcome of patient and persistent good habits, based upon intelligent understanding.

APPENDIX I

THE SCALP COMPRESS

The function of a compress is to induce a lasting, moist warmth, which in turn produces a nervous relaxation (which assists the circulation) and provides an ideal environment for healing and repair. The application of hot fomentations does not provide this effect, since the heat soon passes and the reaction is of chill and depression. By putting *cold* water on the area involved, there is a brief sensation of cold—lasting usually only a matter of seconds—and then a prolonged reaction of warmth, often extending for several hours and until the applied moisture has evaporated.

There are three different ways of applying a scalp compress:

1. By making a close-fitting skull cap of thin cotton or linen material, and a slightly larger cap of doubled or four-ply flannel or other woollen fabric. Soak the thin material in cold water, wring it out and immediately place it upon the scalp, covering with the woollen cap. This may be fastened in position with a tape or by pinching and pinning the slack. It should be comfortably firm, but not tight. The compress should become pleasantly warm in a few minutes, but if it still feels chilly after 10 minutes it should be removed. It may be re-applied an hour

or so later. The compress may safely be left on over-night—provided that it does not stay or become cold—and when taken off in the morning the cotton or linen material should be well washed and rinsed.

2. Take a triangle of cotton or linen, made by cutting diagonally across a large square of material, soak in cold water and wring it out. Place on the scalp with the peak hanging down over the forehead and tie in place with the other two "tails". Fold back the peak and cover with a similar triangle made by *doubling* a square of woollen material diagonally, and apply similarly.

3. For those who have a fair growth of hair over the whole scalp, the inner cap or triangle of cotton or linen is not necessary. It is enough to dip the head in cold water, dry the hair partially and pull on a woollen cap. A single wool beret is usually not quite thick enough to conserve the warmth comfortably, but if covered by a second beret, slightly larger, a very convenient and effective compress is formed.

NOTE WELL: The material which rests against the hair and scalp—whether cotton, linen or a woollen cap—must be thoroughly washed after each application even if it appears quite clean. Cotton and linen should in addition be boiled at least once a week, and any wool which has been against the scalp should be extra thoroughly laundered at the same interval.

Any of these forms of compress should normally be worn throughout the night, but if it produces discomfort it may be safely removed at any time.

APPENDIX II

QUESTIONS AND ANSWERS

Fixatives

1. *Q. You make no mention of dressings of any kind. Are they detrimental to hair growth?*

   A. Dressings which fix the hair, so that it does not require to be combed or brushed, can be discouraging to growth, even if the preparation may be entirely harmless. It is the lack of stimulation by combing and brushing which makes fixatives undesirable. For short hair, adequate tidiness can usually be ensured by applying a moderate amount of plain, cold water two or three times daily, followed by brushing or combing. This encourages scalp circulation and hair growth, besides helping to produce waviness in hair which otherwise might be straight.

Oils

2. *Q. How valuable are the natural oils—such as olive and almond—as hair dressings and as food for the hair?*

   A. It is impossible to feed the hair directly from without. Only through general nutrition and scalp circulation can the follicles be properly supplied, and so enabled to produce a good

77

growth of hair. Oil put upon the hair tends to accumulate dust and scalp debris, which is obviously undesirable. In addition, the edible oils are liable to attract the attention of microscopic forms of life—parasitic or fungal—and may lead to quite serious complications. If the hair is genuinely lacking in natural oil, and until such time as the scalp is in a fit state to provide adequate supplies, a very sparing amount of lanolin is probably the safest substance to improve its appearance. This "wool grease" is very similar to the sebum of human hair, but as ordinarily marketed it usually contains admixtures of other substances to soften it, and which may be unwelcome.

When to cut

3. *Q. Is there any benefit to be derived from cutting the hair during certain phases of the moon?*
A. It is over 50 years since this suggestion was first put to us, and our observation since then has failed to reveal the least effect, beneficial or otherwise. This is hardly surprising, since the point at which a hair is cut has usually been dead for at least some days, and often for months before. Assuming that the individual brushes his hair regularly, the small additional disturbance to the scalp produced by the barber is neither here nor there. When or how the hair is cut seems to have not the least bearing upon the health of the hair or upon its future growth.

Waving

4. *Q. Is curling the hair with hot rollers, by chemical waving or by water setting to be preferred?*

A. The same factors apply here as in the previous question. So far as the continuing hair growth is concerned, these treatments can only have an effect if they are grossly over-applied. That is, an excess of chemical or of heat upon the scalp might do permanent injury to the follicles. A lesser degree of excess might make the hair shaft unsightly, but only such mechanical effects as the tugging can directly influence the follicles, and that is more likely to be beneficial than harmful. Both heat and chemicals obviously introduce an element of risk which is absent with water setting.

Length

5. *Q. Is it known what causes hair to stop growing at apparently predetermined lengths?*

A. If the question refers to the differing qualities of growth on different parts of the body, and under normal conditions, then one can only point to the enormous complexity of hereditary factors. In the evolutionary structure, the first specialised protection produced by the skin appears to have been the scale—as we see today on fishes. The next major development was the feather, which characterises the birds. Hair, which is the special achievement of the mammals, is of similar material to scales and feathers, and is produced in a basically similar way. By and large, the length and closeness of hairs on any part of the body seems to be related to the amount of protection required by the underlying tissues and structures. Hairs and nails are essentially protective outgrowths from the skin, and beyond that fairly obvious fact the field is open for every kind of theory.

But if the question refers to the progressive shortening of hair in *alopecia*, it is the diminished vitality of the follicle which is the major factor. The life-expectation of the active follicle is progressively reduced as the condition deteriorates, and obviously a follicle which is productive for only a few months cannot make as long a hair as one which is vigorously active for several years. As each follicle withers and is replaced by another, the life of each generation has a direct bearing on the length of hair emanating from that spot.

Greasy Scalp

6. *Q. Is the cause known of the over-activity of the sebaceous glands in alopecia seborrhoea?*

A. The over-activity of the sebaceous glands is responsible. *Seborrhoea* is not an entity which has an existence apart from this hypersecretion. That may seem like a mere play on words, but too often it is assumed that *seborrhoea* is a disease which happens to strike the individual, and causes his sebaceous glands to over-produce. In truth, the over-secretion is probably the result of several causes which happen to combine within the individual. It is extremely rare, if not completely unknown, for a bodily disorder to result from a single cause. In *seborrhoea*, the most frequently-met factors are these: The condition of the bloodstream, the vigour and resiliency of the blood-vessels, the tone (the degree of tension) in the muscles of the neck and in the scalp, the possibility of direct injury to the controlling nerves, or of pressure upon them due to deranged structures in the neck.

In most cases, the sebaceous glands seem to be performing a useful—even if untidy—measure of elimination, helping to rid the system of wastes left in the tissues by a sluggish and inadequate blood supply. It therefore follows that any attempt to cure the *seborrhoea* by purely local applications—which fail to improve the blood supply both in quality and in quantity, or to relieve distressed nerves—is illogical and is bound to fail. Treatment by medication may succeed in depressing the local activity, but it is "treatment by misunderstanding" and the long-term effects must be unwholesome. Understanding and the patient removal of causes give the only hope of real cure.

Coincidence

7. *Q. Is it possible to have severe seborrhoea without any accompanying alopecia?*

A. An infinity of complication and combination in disease is possible. As we have noted in the previous answer, disease had no true entity and any abnormal condition can be given a variety of different names, according to the inclination of the individual diagnostician. Sebum and hair are produced by adjacent, but histologically differentiated, structures. Both may be equally disturbed in their functions by a general disorder, or there may be any degree of difference in their respective responses to a particular blood deficiency or nervous strain. There is no anatomical or pathological reason why annoying *seborrhoea* and disfiguring *alopecia* should occur or persist in unison.

Antiseptic Soap

8. *Q. In cases of* **seborrhoea,** *why does the hair become smaller in diameter and the hair roots become shorter and atrophied, even when the scalp is washed daily with antiseptic soap?*

A. The hair stalk becomes thinned, and its follicle diminished, because nutrition has been cut down. Only if the antiseptics in the soap are unusually powerful—for example derived from coal-tar—could they have any marked effect on the situation, and then it would be a detrimental one. It could conceivably injure the follicles, but most probably the soap has no appreciable influence, except that it incidentally encourages the cleansing, rubbing and loosening of the scalp.

Unusual Seborrhoea?

9. *Q. Why is it possible to have a loose scalp, good health and good circulation, and yet suffer from* **alopecia seborrhoea**?

A. Such a combination of circumstances is a rarity, yet it can occur. The most likely cause is that something has recently caused a radical disturbance to the general nutrition—and it could be a physical or an emotional factor. Otherwise, the most probable explanation is that there has been some injury to the neck region, so that the nervous controls to the scalp have been upset. The treatment called for must obviously be determined by the primary cause, as well as by the constitution of the patient in each individual case.

The Beard

10. *Q. Why does the hair of the beard never moult, and is it true that men who have never shaved have softer hair in the beard?*

A. The first part of the question contains an inaccurate implication. Bald patches in the beard are not a rarity, and each follicle has its limited span of activity, just as on the scalp. However, it is quite true that noticeable absence of hair growth is far less common in the beard than on the scalp. Partly this seems to be due to the effect of the sex hormones, which play a significant part in the development and vigour of hair growth on various areas of the body. In women, hair growth on the face is normally only in the form of the lightest down, whereas on the scalp it often has far greater vigour— and for many more years—than in the male. In men, hair growth on the face begins at puberty, and quite often becomes stronger here with the passage of years, while the growth on the scalp weakens. (This has led some commentators to suggest—somewhat fancifully—that baldness is a sign of virility.)

Another probable factor in maintaining beard vigour despite scalp baldness is the active and frequent movement of the jaw. This encourages free blood circulation and looseness of the skin, whereas limited circulation and tightness of the scalp are prevalent causes of baldness.

The effect of shaving is widely misunderstood. Unshaven, every hair retains its natural very fine, silky tip, and as it grows the length gives a flexibility, so that there is nothing to give a sensation of rigidity or scratchiness on contact. But just as a cornstalk, which has a feathery tip and sways gracefully in the slightest breeze, leaves a hard, cruelly sharp stubble when the reaper has passed, so the hairs of the beard seem to gain stiffness and thickness when cut short. Hairs can be caused to coarsen by the irritating effect of various penetrating substances reaching the skin, but neither the massaging effect of razor or shaver nor the application of shaving soap will make any appreciable difference in this respect.

Night-caps

11. *Q. Is there any connection between the fact that in the past men rarely suffered from baldness, and the fact that they habitually wore night-caps?*
A. Someone has said somewhere that if you wish to make an utterly untenable assertion, you should introduce it with the words: "It is universally agreed by those who have devoted their lives to a study of the subject that . . ." Socrates, Julius Caesar and Shakespeare come immediately to mind as examples of historical personages whose portraits have been passed down to us, and whose scalps appear to have given up the struggle. Of course, we cannot be sure that they wore night-caps. Coming down to more modern times, and to personages about whose personal habits we have fuller information, perhaps the questioner would care to study portraits in their later years of such famous night-cap addicts as President Taft,

King Edward VII, Viscount Grey, Cardinal New-
man, William E. Carpenter, Eric Linklater, and
Sir Winston Churchill.

Magnetism

12. *Q. Does cutting the hair with magnetised scissors
increase its growth?*
A. Magnetised scissors are a confounded nui-
sance, since they attract tiny ferrous metal
particles, which interfere with the smoothness
of the cut and ruin the edge. They are therefore
unlikely to be used by any self-respecting
professional hairdresser. In inexperienced hands,
any kind of scissors are likely to be used with a
less deft touch, and the hair is apt to be repeatedly
tugged during cutting operations. Hence, magnetised scissors may be associated with a slight,
just possibly perceptible, improvement in the
vitality of the scalp!

Fashion

13. *Q. When fashion dictates that women should cut
their hair short, does this increase their liability
to baldness?*
A. The length at which hair is cut is of very
little significance compared with other factors,
but longer hair usually puts a greater pull on the
follicles, and is more at the mercy of wind and
weather: both of these effects are beneficial
to scalp vitality. Otherwise, the difference

between short hair and long is a matter of the attention it receives, by way of brushing, combing, washing and styling. If it is more often and more vigorously brushed and combed, and more regularly cleansed, this is likely to improve the condition of scalp and of hair growth. If it receives less such attention, or is immobilised with lacquers or other fixatives, it may suffer from inactivity. The less active the attention given to the hair, the more is deterioration to be expected.

Damp Hair

14. *Q. I am only* 27, *yet have very thin hair on the crown of my head, and the hair at the front is receding. I cannot understand the latter occurrence, as the front "fringe" of my hair is wetted at least three times a day with cold water when I wash.*

A. Although the benefits of applying cold water to the scalp have been repeatedly referred to in this book, merely damping a small area several times a day is not what we have in mind. A generally tight or thin scalp, or a tense neck, may easily prevent an adequate circulation from reaching the devitalised parts, despite any local application. In all cases, it is not the application of cold water which produces any benefit, but the *response* of the living tissues to that cold. If the scalp is vigorously worked upon, after the cold water is applied, an improved circulation may be looked for, and the response may also be expected to improve from week to week. But the comparatively passive damping of the "fringe" may do nothing more than chill that area, and still further depress the circulation. It can have no real effect at all upon the scalp at the crown of the head.

Treatments

15. *Q. I have had three doses of "Violet Ray" treatment at intervals of two months. Is it worth persevering with this? I have also obtained lotions and ointments, and have been advised not to rub the hair vigorously, as that would damage or break off the new hairs. But my hair continues to fall out—without any perceptible replacement.*

A. "Violet Ray" may be nothing more than a mildly spectacular form of gentle electrical stimulation, with neither greater nor lesser effect than would be produced by combing, brushing or stroking the scalp. It is probably harmless, and equally probably almost useless. However, popular terminology often misapplies the name "Violet Ray" to what is really artificial sunlight, or *ultra*-violet radiation, and this can be distinctly valuable—as noted in Chapter VI. However, applications as infrequently as once in two months are unlikely to produce much effect, and one or two sessions per week would be a more reasonable dosage. (Always, it should be stressed that it is *not* necessary to produce a tan in order to benefit from sunlight—real or artificial—and that a sunburn with painful redness should be avoided entirely. Care and moderation are essential.)

As to the lotions and ointments, and the advice not to rub too briskly, we would advise you to scrap the lot. At the same time, it is not advisable to treat the hair violently. Instead, the fingers should carry the hair *and the surface tissues* of the scalp with them. The "rubbing" really occurs under the surface of the skin, between the different layers of the scalp. This is the "friction" which has a real physiological significance. Such kneading of the scalp has quite a different effect from rubbing the hair alone, which might temporarily increase the baldness of a thin, undernourished scalp.

Nerve Trouble

16. *Q. About six months ago my hair began to fall out, and then grew in much stronger. Recently it has begun to fall out again* **rapidly.** *Would the methods you outline help, and can you give me any idea of the cause?*

A. The sequence described sounds suspiciously like the kind of disturbance touched upon under the heading of "Neuritis". Even when it occurs only in a small area, neuritis may have quite

serious systemic implications, and if it has
affected a large portion of the scalp—as your
description suggests—advice should be sought
about the general health. No self-applied local
reatment is likely to help, and professional
guidance is essential.

Dressings

17. *Q. Do you agree with the theory that glycerine
should be used as a dressing for greasy hair,
and olive oil for dry hair?*

A. We believe that healthy hair requires no such
dressings, and that unhealthy hair may be
further deteriorated by applications of such
far-from-inert fluids. Both substances mentioned
are capable of chemical change, and both may
encourage the proliferation of fungal or parasitic
micro-organisms. It is true that some particularly unruly heads of hair demand a great
deal of attention—particularly just after soapy
washing or shampooing. By damping the hair
sufficiently often it can be kept in place, and this
procedure is entirely beneficial to the scalp,
most probably tending to correct whichever of
the disorders mentioned above has been prevalent. (For *occasional* use, where social demands
are exceptional, it may be permissible to use a
fixative based on a vegetable gum such as tra-
gacanth. This is usually marketed as "non-
oily brilliantine" or as "setting lotion", with a

small admixture of dye and scent. Ordinarily, this brushes out of the hair quite completely once it has dried, and produces no clogging effect such as results from the application of glycerine or oil.)

Shampooing

18. *Q. Which soap or shampoo do you recommend for regular use?*

A. Much depends upon the water which is available for washing. If the supply is moderately soft, there seems to be nothing better than a mild toilet soap—preferably undyed, unmedicated, and unscented—and rinsed out thoroughly afterwards. Where the piped water supply is hard, there are several possibilities. Rain-water is probably best, but not at all easy to obtain in many situations. There are also soaps made from ingredients more costly than usual, and with more elegant chemistry, which do not produce a scum and which are claimed to be much milder on the skin. Finally, there are the shampoos, which are closely related to domestic detergents. Formerly, this was not so, but the modern synthetic detergents are so much more effective, and so much less costly to produce, than the old-fashioned shampoos that they have virtually swept them off the market. Detergents are not necessarily harmful, but so far there is none which the makers can guarantee to be harmless to all skins. "Baby shampoo" is probably the safest variety, but even it should be discarded if there is any suspicion of irritation after use. For many people, who have to contend with a very hard water, the easiest method is to use ordinary soap and to clear the resultant scum with a rinse of water to which lemon-juice or vinegar has been added.

Hormones

19. *Q. You have mentioned hormones as a possible factor in baldness. Is it not possible that modern techniques of hormone therapy could counter the effects of an excess or deficiency in the patient, and so restore a healthy hair growth?*

A. The picture given by the question appears reasonable, but it is over-simplified and makes the considerable assumption that a pathological hormone disturbance may exist without any other disorder. This is not our clinical finding. As noted in connection with various conditions throughout this book, it is extremely rare for any bodily ailment to be due to a single cause. It is conceivable that massive dosages of an appropriate biological preparation could stimulate hair growth despite nutritional deficiencies; but it would entail the serious probability of robbing other, more vital, tissues. This quite apart from the near-certainty of producing awkward sexual manifestations.

It is essential to preserve a sense of proportion in these matters, and to recognise that a deficiency of hair-growth on the scalp is trivial when compared with a disturbance of personality or of vital functioning.

Further Advice

20. *Q. If I sent you full details of my hair problem, would you let me have explicit postal instructions for home treatment? I am prepared to pay any reasonable fee.*

A. The suggestions and advice given in this book represent the safe and practical limits of what can be offered to an unseen patient. The information which a patient can supply about his or her own case may appear to be complete, but it cannot provide the vital background which a practitioner gathers at a personal interview and examination. If you feel the need of more specific guidance than given here, we shall be happy to put you in touch with a practitioner familiar with the Kingston System of treatment.

Assurance

21. *Q. Is it genuinely possible for home treatment alone to overcome incipient baldness? Could compresses be safely used without first having a personal consultation?*

A. The great majority of scalp and hair disorders can be treated safely and effectively at home by the methods outlined in this book. A memorable confirmation of the value of home treatment occurred some years when James C. Thomson was discussing some adjustment of his car with a garage mechanic. Quite suddenly the mechanic demanded: "What do you think of that, Mr. Thomson?" and thrust forward a healthy head of hair for inspection. Mildly surprised, J.C.T. made a quick examination, and found nothing unusual. It appeared to be a perfectly normal growth. He said so, and asked what the owner had in mind. In obvious astonishment, the mechanic exclaimed: "Don't you remember I was bald last year? All this grew out of your book!"

IMPORTANT NOTICE

It is regretted that it is impracticable to give detailed personal advice by post. The general principles of the Kingston System have been fully explained in these pages and individual advice can be given only after personal consultation and examination.

Enquiries to: The Secretary, Kingston Clinic, Edinburgh, 9.

Other recommended reading . . .

THE WOMAN'S BOOK OF NATURAL BEAUTY

Anita Guyton's delightful harvest of pure and simple beauty preparations to pamper and improve your body. Fruit, herbs, flowers and vegetables grown at home or gathered from the wild and items from the kitchen store cupboard such as milk, eggs and yeast can all be used in a delightful and delicious series of beauty preparations for the face, hair, hands and body. Look, feel and smell wonderful using only natural ingredients gleaned from garden, meadow and kitchen. The toiletries in this book — many of which are the author's own recipes whilst others have been in her family for generations — are fun and inexpensive to make, and a joy to use, yet, more importantly, give excellent results.

ROYAL JELLY
A GUIDE TO NATURE'S RICHEST HEALTH FOOD

The food of Queens — queen bees to be specific. Specially produced by bees, this super food is capable of turning a perfectly ordinary chrysalis into that magnificent specimen — the Queen Bee. **Irene Stein,** a health and beauty expert, has been actively involved in research into Royal Jelly for over twelve years. In this easy-to-read volume she explains the many health-giving properties of this unique food including: increased alertness; calmness and efficiency; tip-top bodily fitness; shining hair; glowing complexion; strong nails and increased resistance to disease. Used regularly by such celebrities as Sebastian Coe, Cliff Richard, Joe Brown and Barbara Cartland, this remarkable substance really IS nature's richest food.

NATURAL BEAUTY
RADIANT GOOD LOOKS THE HEALTHY WAY

Carol Hunter. Health and beauty are synonymous. Beginning with the crucial importance of a proper diet, author deals with skin care, beauty problems (including treatments for acne, dandruff, wrinkles and facial hair), care of feet, hands, teeth and hair, slimming (based on a seven-day wholefood diet), and home-made cosmetics. Beauty mirrors certain qualities that have nothing to do with the features people are born with. These qualities originate in an inner radiance which is well within the reach of everyone. Looking good is feeling good and looking good brings with it the added bonus of a healthy body and a peaceful, relaxed mind!